MARTIN LUTHER KING, JR.

DIANE PATRICK

MARTIN LUTHER KING, JR.

Franklin Watts
New York • London • Toronto • Sydney • 1990
A First Book

Cover photo courtesy of Magnum Photo (Bob Adelman)

Photographs courtesy of: Life Picture Service: pp. 2 (Francis Miller),
23 bottom (Don Uhrbrock), 39 (P. Schutzer), 47 top (Robert Kelley),
47 bottom (Francis Miller); Photo Researchers: pp. 8, 37 (both Bruce Roberts),
60 top (Mark Chester); Flip Schulke: p. 12; UPI/Bettmann: pp. 14, 20,
44 top, 55 bottom, 60 bottom, 61; Morehouse College: p. 19; Alabama
Bureau of Tourism: pp. 23 top, 62; Boston University Photo Service: p. 25;
Magnum Photo: pp. 28, 55 top (both Bob Adelman); Black Star: pp. 44 bottom,
51, 53 (all Charles Moore), 56 (Fred Ward), 58 (Scheler).

Library of Congress Cataloging-in-Publication Data

Patrick, Diane.
Martin Luther King, Jr. / by Diane Patrick.
p.   cm.—(A First book)
Summary: Traces the life of the Baptist minister, from his early
days and education to his leadership of the civil rights movement.
ISBN 0-531-10892-9
1. King, Martin Luther, Jr., 1929–1968—Juvenile literature.
2. Afro-Americans—Biography—Juvenile literature.   3. Civil rights
workers—United States—Biography—Juvenile literature.
4. Baptists—United States—Clergy—Biography—Juvenile literature.
5. Afro-Americans—Civil rights—Juvenile literature.   [1. King,
Martin Luther, Jr., 1929–1968.   2. Clergy.   3. Civil rights workers.
4. Afro-Americans—Biography.]   I. Title.   II. Series.
E185.97.K5P28   1990   323′.092—dc20
[92]   [B]   89-24800   CIP   AC

CONTENTS

MARTIN LUTHER KING, JR.

*In the South until just a few
decades ago, most public places were
segregated, including washrooms.*

INTRODUCTION

A LEADER EMERGES

◆——◆

Whenever you drink water from a water fountain or get on a bus or train and sit anywhere you like, you really don't have to think about it. You are used to doing these things. You take it for granted that you can do them.

Yet, just a few decades ago, in the southern states of the United States, this was not true for black people. Because of *prejudices,* or dislike of an individual because of a particular group he or she is in, the laws of most of these states required that black people be *segregated,* or separated, from white people as much as possible. On buses and trains, in restaurants, in schools and parks—in all public places, in fact—there were signs reading "White Only" and "Colored Only." ("Colored" and "Negro" were the terms used then to describe black people. Today, non-white people of African descent are referred to as "African-American" or "black." In this book, the term black is used.) If a black person went into a "White" area, he or she would be arrested.

In the late 1950s, a small group of black people decided to protest against this unfair treatment. Eventually, almost all black people in the country were involved in the long, painful struggle to be treated equally. This struggle was called the *civil rights movement.*

Many black people felt that the success of the struggle was important enough to die for. In fact, many did die. They died because they didn't want their children and grandchildren—some of you who are reading this book, for example—to be treated the way they had been. It takes great courage to give up one's life for something one believes in. This is why we remember these people as heroes. We must never forget their sacrifices.

The civil rights movement was an unusual fight. Because of the guidance of Martin Luther King, Jr., it was fought without using violence, though violence was often used to try to stop it.

Martin Luther King, Jr., lived for only thirty-nine years, but in his short lifetime he helped to develop unity among black people and to change the way blacks were treated. He was a remarkable writer and a powerful speaker.

King believed in protesting against unfairness. However, he believed that the protesting must be done without violence, and he taught millions of people how to protest in a nonviolent manner.

During the civil rights movement, King was arrested many times and often faced great physical danger. But he remained dedicated to his cause. His achievements were recognized worldwide, and he won many awards. Martin Luther King, Jr., was one of the most important leaders of the civil rights movement in the United States.

CHAPTER ONE

EARLY YOUTH AND EDUCATION

◆◆◆

Background • It was Tuesday, January 15, 1929. On a tree-lined street in Atlanta, Georgia, stood a large, friendly house. Inside the house on that cold, cloudy day, a baby boy was born.

The baby's parents named him Martin Luther King, Jr., after his father. There was already another child in the family, a little girl named Christine. But Martin was the first son.

Martin's father, the Reverend Martin Luther King, Sr., was a minister. Everyone called him Daddy King. He was a kind, strong man. Martin's mother was Alberta Williams King; she was a schoolteacher. Her father, the Reverend Adam Daniel Williams, was a minister, too. He lived in the same house with Martin's parents and was the person who started Ebenezer Baptist Church, one of the biggest black churches in the city of Atlanta.

Daddy King's parents had been sharecroppers, which means they worked on a white farmer's land picking his crops. Although they worked very hard and very long hours, they never made enough money to buy land of their own.

Ebenezer Baptist Church,
Atlanta, Georgia

Daddy King loved his parents very much, but he was determined not to live the way they had. So he worked days and studied at night, and slowly he became educated and a minister. At the time of Martin's birth, Daddy King was the head of Ebenezer Baptist Church.

Early Childhood • Martin was born at the beginning of the Great Depression. During this time, a lot of people were out of work all over the country. Companies could not afford to hire workers. Many people could not afford homes or food. It was a very sad time for America.

Still, Martin's family was a happy one. They were not rich, but they were not poor, either. The children had music lessons and nice clothes to wear, and they had good friends. Their parents' friends always made a big fuss over them, especially in church. It was like a big, loving family.

"We Can't Play Together Anymore" • When Martin was six years old, he received some bad news from one of his close friends. The boy, who was white, told Martin that his father had forbidden him to play with Martin any longer. Martin was shocked. He ran home and told his mother about the incident. He asked her if she could explain what had happened.

Upon hearing his story, Martin's mother realized that the time had come to tell her son about slavery and freedom, prejudice and segregation. This is a story that all black parents must eventually tell their children.

Martin was a very bright boy and soon began to understand. He had seen the signs downtown that read "Whites Only" and "Colored Only." He realized that there were no white families where he lived, and no white children in his school. He realized that the places where blacks were allowed to go were not as fancy or well-kept as places where whites went.

This was Martin's first experience with prejudice. After his parents told Martin a little about black history in America, including slavery, they told him that, in spite of this, he should never feel that he was lower than other people. "You are as good as anyone," they said.

Martin's parents set a good example for him in this regard. Daddy King was a strong man who had fought for an education, for a good life for his family, and for what he thought was right. He was afraid of no one.

Riding the Bus • Martin did not grow very tall as he got older, and he looked young for his age. But he was very polite and had a wonderful speaking voice. He also spoke excellent English. He read a lot of books and wrote well. He was so good at his schoolwork that he was even skipped several grades.

When he was fourteen, he was chosen to represent his school in a speech contest in another part of Georgia. The speech he wrote was called "The Negro and the Constitution." Without using any notes, he made this speech at the contest and won second prize. He was very excited and proud.

After the contest, Martin and his teacher sat together on a bus as they traveled back home to Atlanta. It was a long trip. In those days, according to the law, whites rode in the front of buses, and blacks rode in the back. The buses had little signs reading WHITES FORWARD, COLORED REAR. If all of the "White" seats were filled and more whites got on, the seated blacks would have to get up and give the whites their seats.

Suddenly, the bus driver began yelling to Martin and his teacher to get up. Two white passengers were getting on.

Martin's teacher didn't move fast enough for the driver. He began to curse at them both, and Martin was horrified. No one had ever spoken to him that way before! He wanted to protest the driver's rudeness. But his teacher appeared scared, so he got up. He realized that if he did not, they might be arrested.

Martin and his teacher stood for the rest of the long ride. All Martin could think about was how his speech was a joke. He had never been angrier in his life, and he never forgot the incident.

By the time Martin was in high school, he was one of the most popular boys in his class. He dressed well, and he was a good dancer. But he was also one of the best students. His grades were so good that he was given a chance to skip ninth and twelfth grades and begin college early.

College Days • The college Martin chose was Morehouse College in Atlanta. Morehouse was an all-black college famous for its high academic standards.

A few weeks after beginning classes at Morehouse, Martin noticed he was falling behind with the work. He frequently could not understand what the other students were talking about in class. The homework was difficult for him to do. One of his teachers noticed this and arranged for him to take an achievement test. The test results showed that Martin was four years behind in reading!

At first, Martin was sure there had been a mistake. Hadn't his grades in high school been among the best?

Then one of his professors explained it. The standards at the high school Martin had attended had been low. Because the students were all black, the school board hadn't thought that it was important for them to have a quality education.

Martin was discouraged, but his father convinced him not to give up. So Martin began doing extra work to raise his reading level. By the end of his second year, he had caught up with his class. He joined the glee club and participated in speech contests and other college activities. He was even a member of the football team.

Choosing a Career • At first, Martin didn't want to be a minister. He wanted to be a doctor. But he found his science courses difficult, so he changed his major to sociology, the study of the way people live and act in groups.

This tribute to King stands outside Morehouse College in Atlanta.

One summer, Martin and a group of students traveled to Connecticut for a summer job. The group chose Martin as their devotional leader. In this role, he led them in prayer and helped them with their problems. He enjoyed the experience and was impressed by the positive way they responded to his advice.

In Martin's junior year at Morehouse, his father allowed him to deliver a trial sermon at Ebenezer Baptist Church. It was very successful, and as a result, Martin was given the right to preach there. He became assistant pastor to his father and decided to make religion his life's work.

Religious Studies • Martin studied for his degree in religion at Crozer Theological Seminary in Pennsylvania. At Crozer, Martin again did very well. He read many books about philosophy and religion. One of the famous people he read about was the Indian leader Mohandas K. Gandhi. India had been ruled by England for many years. In 1947, with Gandhi's leadership, the people of India were able to form their own government and become an independent country.

Mahatma Gandhi and some of his followers

Gandhi believed that if laws were unfair, people should not obey them. They should also be willing to go to jail for disobeying them.

Gandhi further believed that although people should protest unfair treatment, they must never use violence. He felt that in this way, people could touch the hearts of their enemies and thereby change them. He called this method of protest *passive resistance*. By practicing these beliefs, Gandhi led a successful, and generally bloodless, revolution of his people.

Martin was fascinated by the idea of a revolution without violence. He had no idea that one day that very type of revolution would change his life and the lives of millions of others as well.

Martin's professors at Crozer were very impressed with him. They recommended that he continue his studies toward one more degree—a doctorate, which is the highest academic degree a person can earn. He took their advice and began his doctoral studies at Boston University.

CHAPTER TWO

MARRIAGE AND EARLY CAREER

◆ ◆

One day, a friend introduced Martin to a young music student named Coretta Scott. Coretta also went to school in Boston. On their first date, Martin told Coretta that she had the qualities he wanted in a wife! Coretta was a bit surprised at his boldness, but she agreed to see him again. On June 18, 1953, they were married by Martin's father at the home of Coretta's parents.

In March 1954, Martin was invited to become the pastor of the Dexter Avenue Baptist Church in Montgomery, Alabama. He wasn't sure how to respond to the invitation. He and Coretta enjoyed their quiet life in the North. Coretta wanted to stay and pursue a career in music. They were not happy about the idea of moving back to the segregated South. But the U. S. Supreme Court had just

Left: *Dexter Avenue Baptist Church.*
Below: *King preaching to his congregation.*

decided, in what was to become a very famous case called *Brown* v. *Board of Education,* that segregation in public schools was unconstitutional—against federal law. Martin knew that this would be the beginning of important changes for black people, so he decided that he wanted to be in the South to help. He accepted the invitation.

Settling Down • Martin preached at Dexter almost every Sunday for a whole year. Everyone enjoyed the inspiration he provided. But Dexter was a quiet church that was not always well attended.

Still, this worked out well for Martin. It allowed him to spend time at home with his new bride and to work on his doctoral dissertation. (A dissertation is a long paper that a student must write to be considered for a doctoral degree.)

Martin was awarded his doctorate from Boston University in June 1955. This meant that he could now be called "Dr. King." On November 17, 1955, Martin and Coretta's first child, Yolanda Denise, was born. Martin and Coretta looked forward to watching their daughter grow. They had no idea that in a few weeks, their lives would change rather dramatically.

King gets his doctorate from Boston University.

CHAPTER THREE

THE MONTGOMERY BUS BOYCOTT

◆━━◆━━◆

On Thursday evening of December 1, 1955, a black woman named Mrs. Rosa Parks was on her way home from work in Montgomery, Alabama. She was tired from her long day at the downtown department store.

After work, Mrs. Parks had caught the bus to go home. It was cold outside. The bus was crowded. The only available seats were those directly behind the "Whites Only" seats. Mrs. Parks sat down in one of these.

After the last "White" seat was taken, one man, who was white, was left standing. The bus driver looked back and saw Mrs. Parks and three other black people sitting in the row next to her.

"All right, you folks, I want those seats," the driver called out to them. Even though the standing passenger needed only one seat, Montgomery's segregation laws stated that no black person was allowed to sit in the same row as a white person. Therefore, all four of them would have to stand in order to allow one white man to sit.

The three black passengers who were sitting next to Mrs. Parks got up and moved to the back. But Mrs. Parks remained seated.

"Look, woman, I told you I wanted the seat. Are you going to stand up?" the driver asked.

Calmly and quietly, Mrs. Parks answered: "No."

"If you don't stand up, I'm going to have you arrested," the driver responded.

Still calm, Mrs. Parks told him to go right ahead, but that she was not going to move. The driver got off the bus and went to phone the police.

A policeman arrived and told Mrs. Parks to get up. She replied, "I didn't think I should have to stand. Why do you push us around?" The policeman said, "I don't know, but the law is the law, and you're under arrest."

Soon after this, a black person who had seen Mrs. Parks being arrested told the story to Mr. E. D. Nixon, a black community leader for whom Mrs. Parks had worked as a secretary. Mr. Nixon went right over to the police station and asked Mrs. Parks if he could use her case to try to bring an end to segregation on the buses in Montgomery. Mrs. Parks agreed.

Mrs. Rosa Parks, whose actions led to the Montgomery bus boycott and an end to segregation on the buses in the South

"Don't ride the bus on Monday" • The black community leaders had an idea. What if blacks boycotted the buses for one day? (A *boycott* is when a large group of people refuse to buy something or use certain services for an agreed length of time.) If they refused to ride on the buses for one day, perhaps the bus company would agree to treat black riders more fairly.

There were about 50,000 black people in the city of Montgomery. They all had to be notified of the plan. In Montgomery, there were a lot of community organizations and churches. The members volunteered to spread the word and to help.

Fifty-two thousand notices were typed and printed by a teacher and two students at Alabama State College. The notices read:

> *Another Negro woman has been arrested and thrown into jail because she refused to get up out of her seat on the bus for a white person to sit down. Please, children and grown-ups, don't ride the bus at all on Monday. Please stay off all buses Monday.*

Students helped to distribute the notices.

The boycott was a success. On Monday, December 5, 1955, not one black person was seen riding the buses in Montgomery.

"We must not hate our opponents" • That night, a meeting was held in a church. King, still fairly new in town, had been invited to be one of the speakers. Thousands of black people attended—so many that they were lined up outside for four blocks! When King's turn to speak came, he said he agreed that the black people must fight against injustice. But he suggested using an unusual weapon. "We must use the weapon of protest. But we must not hate our opponents," he warned. "We must protest with courage, dignity, and Christian love."

The crowd liked King's ideas. After he spoke, they gave him a standing ovation.

The people then took a vote on whether to continue the boycott until the bus company agreed to a fairer system of seating on the buses. The vote was unanimous in favor of continuing. The boycott would probably last only three or four days anyway, they thought, because black leaders were scheduled to meet with bus company officials to try to work out an agreement.

Leading the Boycott • The black community leaders decided to form a group to direct the boycott. They called the group the Montgomery Improvement Association. To his surprise, King was elected president of the group; he was new and young, and they liked the way he spoke.

At first, King was hesitant to accept the position. He was a new father and a new pastor and didn't know if he would have the time to deal with such a big project. He also knew that it might become dangerous. But he really wanted to help, and finally he agreed.

Soon, King became known as the main spokesperson for the boycott. He was very mature for a twenty-seven-year-old, and people were impressed with his patience and his optimism. He continued to guide them with his wisdom. Sometimes, he would tell them stories about Gandhi. Other times, he would tell them about the sacrifices he and others were making to promote the cause of blacks. After the speeches, the group would sing songs of freedom. They always left the meetings feeling hopeful.

Staying Off the Bus • The bus boycott, as it dragged on, was very hard on the black people of Montgomery. They had to walk in the rain, the heat, and the cold. People with cars tried to give rides to those who needed them. In the evenings, they continued to hold regular meetings at their local churches to plan strategies and to organize activities. By helping each other and sticking together, they believed that they could make a difference.

As the bus boycott continued, some whites became frustrated and angry. To intimidate the black people, the police were ordered to arrest any black person who committed any small violation at all. King and the other black leaders received obscene phone calls. One day, King was arrested for driving too fast. For the first time, he was put in jail. Although he was soon released without bond, the experience made him realize how dangerous the course he was taking could be. But he decided that he must not be afraid. The struggle was too important.

"There will be others to take my place" • A few nights later, King was attending a church meeting. Coretta was at home with the baby and a friend. They were sitting in the front room. Suddenly, they heard what sounded like a brick striking the floor on the front porch. As they ran toward the back room, an explosion tore through the house. Fortunately, no one was hurt.

King rushed home. He said to his neighbors who were gathered outside, "If I am stopped, our work will not stop—for what we are doing is right. Go home and sleep calm as I and my family are. Remember that if anything happens to me, there will be others to take my place."

Challenging the Laws • Meanwhile, negotiations were taking place between bus company officials and black leaders. However, the bus company officials would not agree to any compromises. The black leaders were surprised at the lack of cooperation. Eventually, they decided that since the bus company would not agree to even their very minor requests, they should challenge the state laws that allowed bus segregation to continue. The Supreme Court decision in the *Brown* v. *Board of Education* case, they realized, could be the basis for a lawsuit alleging that segregation on buses was also unconstitutional. They hired attorneys, filed the lawsuit, and waited for a judicial decision.

The Country Sees • By this time, national newspapers and radio and television stations were becoming interested in the boycott. They sent reporters and photographers to bring back stories and pictures of what they saw. For the first time, many people in other parts of the country learned of the racial problems in the South.

Victory • Finally, on November 13, 1956, the U. S. Supreme Court ruled that segregation on the Montgomery buses was indeed unconstitutional. The black people then voted to call off the boycott. It had been intended for one day and had lasted for over eleven months!

CHAPTER FOUR

BECOMING A LEADER

◆◆◆

King was becoming quite well known. His speeches were strong and inspiring, and he was spoken of as a leader of the black people. Many newspaper and magazine articles were written about him. His picture even appeared on the cover of *Time* magazine. He was asked to speak at meetings and events all across the country. He even began writing a book about the Montgomery bus boycott.

Several months after the end of the boycott, King and some other black leaders formed an organization that came to be called the Southern Christian Leadership Conference, or SCLC. Most of the organization's leaders were ministers. The SCLC's main goals were to teach blacks how to participate in protests against segregation and to coordinate the activities of various protest groups in the South.

King Is Attacked • In 1958, King traveled to New York to speak in several churches. *Stride Toward Freedom,* his book about the Montgomery bus boycott, had just been published. One Saturday, he was in a Harlem bookstore autographing copies of the book. Suddenly, a woman named Izola Curry came up to him. "Is this Martin Luther King?" she asked. "Yes," King said. At that, she pulled out a very sharp letter opener from her bag and stabbed him in the upper left chest. King did not lose consciousness and remained calm and motionless until an ambulance came. The letter opener stayed in his chest the whole time.

King was taken to Harlem Hospital, where he was successfully operated on to remove the letter opener. It took several hours to complete the surgery. King did not realize it then, but the letter opener had been right next to the aorta, the large vein that carries blood from the heart to the rest of the body. If there had been any movement— even if King had sneezed—the aorta would have been punctured, and he would have died.

The surgery left King with a scar, in the shape of a cross, right over his heart. The woman who had stabbed him was found mentally unable to stand trial and was committed to a state hospital. King said that he harbored no ill feelings toward her.

The Work Continues • King slowly resumed his usual busy schedule of traveling, making speeches, demonstrating in protests, and preaching. He spoke to anyone—from local officials to the president of the United States—whom he felt could provide assistance in the struggle against segregation.

King's busy schedule forced him to resign from the pastorship of the Dexter Avenue Baptist Church in 1960. In its place, he became co-pastor with his father at Ebenezer. This, he thought, would give him time to work on his many other projects. He also wanted to spend more time with his family, which now included a baby son, Martin Luther King III. But, once again, another development in the civil rights movement would interrupt his plans.

"Why can't we be served here?" • In those days, black people could only be served in restaurants in the South that had signs reading "Colored Only." Four young black men who were college students in Greensboro, North Carolina, decided to protest this unfair treatment. On February 1, 1960, they sat down at a Woolworth's lunch counter, intending not to leave until they were served. They did this even though they knew that protesting could result in their being beaten or arrested.

The four young men were respectful, well dressed, and well spoken. After purchasing some toothpaste and school supplies, they went to the lunch counter and ordered coffee. As they expected, the waitress said, "I'm sorry, but we don't serve colored here."

"But we were just served at other counters. Why can't we be served here?" they asked. No one answered. The four were simply ignored. A half hour later, the store closed, and they left.

What these four students were doing was called a *sit-in*. Over the next few days, thanks to the organizing efforts of the black leaders, there were sit-ins at lunch counters all over the city.

The sit-in at Woolworth's lunch counter

Before long, crowds of whites began to gather at these lunch counters to harass the students. They poured food and hot coffee on them. Sometimes they would yank the students off their seats and beat them. Each time the black students—not the white people—would be arrested for disorderly conduct. But the next day, more students were there to take their places. Many were afraid but did it anyway. News reporters filmed and photographed the events for the entire country to see. Soon students in other segregated cities began to follow the example of the protesting students.

The Student Movement Grows • King was pleased by the fact that young people were taking some responsibility for putting an end to segregation. He realized that young people, with their energy, could be one of the strongest forces in the movement.

King was asked to meet with some student representatives in North Carolina. He suggested that the students there form a group with other students who were involved in the protest. This group. King said, could act as coordinator for the entire project. He promised that the SCLC would be behind them and give them the support they needed.

As a result the students formed an organization they called the Student Non-Violent Coordinating Committee, or SNCC. SNCC organized additional sit-ins and demonstrations at different businesses that practiced segregation.

John F. Kennedy at a meeting of black leaders during the Democratic Convention in 1960

A New President • The year 1960 was a presidential election year. King felt that it would be worthwhile to personally speak to the candidates, Senator John F. Kennedy and Vice President Richard M. Nixon, about the problems in the South. He would outline the country's racial problems and ask each candidate what he would do to help improve things if he became president. After speaking to both men several times, King decided that Kennedy would be more supportive of the civil rights movement.

Kennedy won the election. King and many other people involved with the civil rights movement felt hopeful that President Kennedy would assist them in defeating segregation.

CHAPTER FIVE

MARCHING FOR FREEDOM AND PEACE

◆◆◆

In January 1961, King became the father of another son, Dexter Scott, named after the church where King had preached. In March 1963, his daughter Bernice Albertine was born.

Also in 1963, it was decided that a good place for a demonstration would be Birmingham, Alabama. Blacks considered Birmingham to be the most racially segregated city in the country. The city had even closed its parks, playgrounds, swimming pools, and golf courses rather than comply with a federal order to desegregate public facilities. In addition, there had been many unsolved bombings in black neighborhoods there.

The police commissioner of Birmingham was a man named Eugene ("Bull") Connor. Connor made no secret of the fact that he hated blacks, and he made sure that local segregation laws were strictly followed. As police commissioner, he did nothing to protect blacks. The black people in Birmingham were afraid of Bull Connor.

The Birmingham demonstration was planned in great detail. Black leaders studied Birmingham's city laws and regulations to learn what constituted grounds for arrest. They held meetings all over the country. King went on a national tour to tell people about their plans for Birmingham. He delivered twenty-eight speeches in sixteen cities. He raised funds and recruited volunteers everywhere he went.

King led one of the first demonstrations in Birmingham. As expected, he was arrested and jailed. Local white ministers placed a large advertisement in the local newspaper calling King a troublemaker.

King wanted to respond to this by writing a letter to them. But he had no paper in jail. So he wrote the letter in the margins of the newspaper and on scraps of toilet paper.

In this letter, King explained to the white ministers and to the world why the fight against racism had to begin now. He wrote:

> *For years now I have heard the word "Wait!" . . . . This "Wait" has almost always meant "Never" . . . . Perhaps it is easy for those who have never felt the stinging darts of segregation to*

say, "Wait." But when you have seen hate-filled policemen curse, kick, and even kill your black brothers and sisters; . . . when you seek to explain to your six-year-old daughter why she can't go to the public amusement park that has just been advertised on television . . . then you will understand why we find it difficult to wait.

King's letter was later published as an essay called "Letter From a Birmingham Jail." It was reprinted in dozens of magazines and newspapers all over the world.

The Children Get Involved • After King was released from jail, black leaders began to plan the next phase of the protest. A lot of demonstrations were needed, but retaliation was a very real possibility in Birmingham. People might even lose their jobs. Children, they decided, would be less at risk. When the news reports showed innocent young children being arrested and taken to jail for demonstrating, the entire nation would see how cruel the Birmingham authorities really were.

It was not hard to get children to help in the protests. Parents of black Birmingham schoolchildren from six to eighteen years old were asked to take their children to their local churches to see a film about a student sit-in movement. The film was called "The Nashville Story." Many children came to see the film. Then the children were taught how to act when arrested. They made posters and signs to be carried as they marched. The children were well prepared.

Thursday, May 2, was the date the children were to begin their demonstrations in Birmingham. That morning, King addressed a gathering of children at the Sixteenth Street Baptist Church. He told them how proud he was of them for fighting for their parents and for the future of America.

After his speech, a group of children began to march toward downtown, singing songs of freedom. Police moved in to arrest them, but additional groups of children followed. As their numbers increased over the next four hours, Bull Connor brought in school buses to take them away. By the end of the day, over nine hundred children had been taken to Birmingham jails.

The next day, more than a thousand children stayed out of school to march. This time, Bull Connor brought out the city's police dogs and ordered the city's firemen to turn their water hoses on the children.

On television sets all across the country, people saw the children being knocked down by powerful streams of water from the hoses and chased by snarling police dogs. Newspapers and magazines at home and abroad also reported the events. The federal government grew concerned about how the events would make the United States look to the rest of the world. This was exactly the result King had hoped for.

Right: *Bull Connor leads officers during a mass arrest in Birmingham, Alabama.* Below: *Police use attack dogs against civil rights demonstrators in Birmingham.*

More and more of Birmingham's black population became involved, and the marches grew in size. By Monday, May 6, more than 2,000 demonstrators had been jailed. The jails could not even hold all of the prisoners.

President Kennedy sent a federal aide to Birmingham to set up negotiations between King and the city's business leaders. He asked King and the other leaders what they wanted from the white people of Birmingham. They said they wanted the desegregation of lunch counters in downtown stores—as a beginning. Several days later, the merchants agreed to desegregate lunch counters and hire black workers.

King was pleased with the victory. But some white leaders were angry, and there was much violence directed at the blacks. In addition to rioting, the motel where King was staying and his brother's home were bombed. Federal troops had to be sent in to maintain order. Fortunately, no one was killed.

The President Is Angry • These events led President Kennedy to go on television to ask all Americans to eliminate the practice of segregation from the country. He said that he would ask Congress to pass laws that would give all Americans the right to be served in public places such as hotels, restaurants, theaters, and stores. "No American in 1963 should have to endure denial of this right," he said. King was pleased with President Kennedy's speech. He felt that his people had finally been heard.

As promised, on June 19, 1963, Kennedy delivered a civil rights bill to Congress for passage. This bill banned segregation on all public interstate transportation systems. It allowed the government to start lawsuits that would force school integration and to cut off government funds to any federal program that permitted discrimination. It also contained a provision that helped guarantee the right to vote by declaring that a person who had a sixth-grade education would be presumed to be literate (able to read and write) and could therefore register to vote. Local laws were often designed to prevent blacks from voting.

King and the other civil rights leaders had no intention of letting this bill die in Congress. To show how much they wanted Congress to pass the bill, they decided to organize a huge demonstration in Washington, D.C. Civil rights groups and churches all across the country were to notify people about the demonstration.

The March on Washington • This demonstration, called the March on Washington, took place on August 28, 1963. It was a clear, hot day. Over 250,000 people from all across the country arrived in Washington—as many as 60,000 of them were white. They arrived on more than 30 "freedom" trains and 2,000 chartered "freedom" buses.

Before the speeches began, musical groups entertained the crowd with songs of freedom. Then various civil rights leaders spoke to the crowd and told them and the nation that

Above: *People from all across the country gathered near the Washington Monument for a massive demonstration in Washington.* Right: *King meets with other black leaders at the Lincoln Memorial.*

they were gathered there to show that they wanted freedom for all black Americans.

By then, King was the best-known civil rights leader. The speech he delivered at the March on Washington was broadcast all across the country. It told of his dream that blacks and whites could live together in peace. It was the most famous speech he ever made, and it is called his "I Have a Dream" speech. In it, he said:

> *I have a dream today . . . that one day right there in Alabama, little black boys and black girls will be able to join hands with little white boys and girls as sisters and brothers. I have a dream to-day!*

The March on Washington was the largest demonstration for human rights in the history of the United States. For the first time, many Americans witnessed blacks and whites together, peacefully marching and celebrating their common goals side by side. There were no major disturbances.

The Violence Continues • As exciting as it was, the March on Washington did not immediately result in improvements. With the growth of the civil rights movement, white segregationists in the South became more determined than ever to keep things as they were. The violence increased. There were bombs left on the doorsteps of black homes, and many who demonstrated or worked for the civil rights cause were injured, arrested, or even killed.

Still, the protests and demonstrations continued. The president was asked to give federal protection. Media coverage also increased, allowing the rest of the country—and the world—to see what was going on in the South.

King Is Exhausted • In November 1963, after holding office for less than three years, President Kennedy was shot and killed. Lyndon B. Johnson became the new president, and he urged Congress to pass the civil rights bill quickly in Kennedy's memory.

Meanwhile, King's heavy traveling and speaking schedule took its toll. In the fall of 1964, when he and Coretta returned from a long European speaking tour, he looked so tired that Coretta and his doctor advised him to check into a hospital and have a physical examination. The doctors discovered that King was overweight and suffering from a severe viral infection and high blood pressure.

The Nobel Peace Prize • While King was still resting in the hospital, Coretta received notification that he had won the Nobel Peace Prize. This prize is awarded every year to the person who has made the greatest contribution that year to achieving world peace. The Nobel Prize also came with a financial award of $54,000. Martin Luther King, Jr., was the youngest person ever to receive the prize.

King is awarded the Nobel Prize in Norway.

Many reporters came to interview King. He told them, "History has thrust me into this position. It would be a sign of ingratitude if I did not face my moral responsibility to do what I can in this struggle." Martin felt that receiving the award meant that he would have to work even harder for peace and freedom.

On December 10, 1964, King was presented the Nobel Peace Prize in a formal ceremony at Oslo University in Norway. Coretta King, King's parents, and several of King's aides were there. The king of Norway was also present.

When he accepted the prize, King told the audience that he accepted it on behalf of the entire civil rights movement. He optimistically stated that he had faith in America and in the future of humankind.

Marching to Montgomery • In Alabama, only one in a hundred blacks was allowed to vote. The system there was designed so that blacks would find it very difficult to register to vote. Few blacks could read or write, and they were given tests that were impossible for them to pass. Sometimes, blacks who attempted to register to vote were threatened.

Few Southern blacks could read or write, so they were given tests that were impossible for them to pass. This made them ineligible to vote.

King and the SCLC decided that they would go to Montgomery to try to discuss the voter registration problems with Governor George Wallace. They would march the 54 miles (86.4 km) from Selma to Montgomery, the state capital, where the governor's office was located. Although Governor Wallace had issued an order prohibiting the march, they intended to try it anyway, even if they had to try it more than once.

The leaders decided that King should not be in the first group to march. They knew that there would be violence, and they wanted to attract the public's attention first.

On Sunday, March 7, 1965, 1,500 marchers walked across the Pettus Bridge. State troopers were there waiting for them. "You have two minutes to turn around and go back to your church," they told the marchers. The marchers had decided beforehand that they would not turn around. So they just stopped and stood there.

Then the troop commander ordered the troops to advance. They began pushing and beating the marchers while spraying tear gas. The marchers began running back across the bridge, and over seventy were injured. The troops, who were on horseback, chased the marchers all the way back to their church. Again, camera crews were there to take pictures and film the event. The photos and stories that were printed on the front pages of newspapers shocked people all over the country.

State troopers attack marchers with clubs and tear gas.

This was the result that the black leaders had expected, and they had decided in advance how to react to it. They would flood the White House and Congress with telegrams denouncing the attack. They would also send out requests to several hundred religious leaders and civil rights supporters to come to Selma. On Tuesday, they would again try to march to Montgomery. In the meantime, their lawyers would seek a federal court order preventing any interference with their march.

The Marchers Try Again • On Tuesday, the marchers, with King joining them this time, set out in a second attempt to see the governor. There was still an order barring the march to Montgomery. As the marchers proceeded to cross the Pettus Bridge, they were again stopped by the troops. At that point, King told the troopers that the marchers would begin praying. They knelt, and after prayers were said and songs sung, King turned around and led the marchers back to the church. Some people called King a coward, but he later explained that he had been attempting to show the world how the authorities would not let them conduct a peaceful march.

Meanwhile, President Johnson was growing impatient with the South. He promised that a voting rights proposal would be going to Congress in a few days. He also told Governor Wallace that the state troopers should protect, not attack, peaceful demonstrators seeking to draw attention to their problems.

The March Begins Yet Again • Finally, the federal court ruled that the group had a right to march and that the state troopers must give them protection. On Sunday, March 21, 1965, yet another march from Selma to Montgomery began. This time, King and many of his supporters—black and white—marched the 54 miles. It took five days. There were no attacks, and toward the end of the march, 25,000 people had joined them.

Left: *King marches with the other protestors toward the state capitol.* Below: *Under federal order, state troopers watch as the marchers arrive at the capitol.*

When they arrived in Montgomery, King spoke. After his speech, a group of the leaders went inside the capital to present a petition to Governor Wallace asking him to remove all obstacles to black voter registration in the state of Alabama.

The Voting Rights Act Is Law • The Voting Rights Act was signed into law by President Johnson on August 6, 1965. In a very short time, the number of black voters in the South increased substantially.

President Lyndon Johnson speaks after signing into law the Voting Rights Act.

CHAPTER SIX

LATER YEARS

Despite major gains, King did not stop working to improve conditions for blacks in America. Although he often felt that his life was in danger, he continued to write, make speeches, and assist groups interested in furthering the cause of civil rights. In his travels he visited many poverty-stricken black communities. He began speaking out against discrimination against blacks in housing, schools, and jobs. He also spoke out against the war in Vietnam, because he hated war and killing.

In February 1968, the sanitation workers in Memphis, Tennessee, went on strike. They wanted better working conditions and wages. King and some of his aides went to Memphis for a few days to give their support and assistance

King with wife, children, and parents

to the striking workers. In a speech telling why he came to
help, King said:

> *The question is not what will happen to me if I
> stop to help someone who needs me, but what
> will happen to them if I do not stop? . . . It*

doesn't matter what happens to me now. I've been to the mountaintop and I don't mind. I'm not concerned about what happens to me.

These unselfish words were spoken during the last public speech King would ever make.

The next day, King and his aides worked on plans for a march to support the striking sanitation workers. Just before dinnertime, King stepped onto the second-floor balcony of his room in the Lorraine Motel for a breath of fresh air. One of his aides suggested that King put on a jacket because it was getting chilly.

King turned to go into the room for the jacket. Suddenly, there was a loud, popping sound. King fell to the floor of the balcony. His aides rushed to King's side, but they could see that it was too late—King had been shot in the head. An ambulance came, but there was nothing the doctors could do. Martin Luther King, Jr., was dead.

The news that King had been killed caused an explosion of anger and frustration throughout the country. There were riots in over a hundred cities. King would undoubtedly have been very angry indeed at the violence that took place as a result of his death.

The hunt for King's killer led police to a man named James Earl Ray, a white man who had been in trouble with the law for most of his life. Eventually, Ray was convicted of King's murder and sentenced to many years in jail.

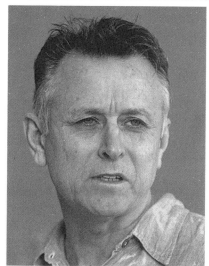

Above: *The balcony at the Lorraine Motel in Memphis, Tennessee, where King was assassinated.* Right: *James Earl Ray, convicted killer of Martin Luther King, Jr.*

Mourners pay tribute to King at his funeral.

A tour guide stands in front of a mural, in the Dexter Avenue Church, dedicated to the life of Martin Luther King, Jr.

A National Holiday • In 1986, the birthday of Dr. Martin Luther King, Jr. became a national holiday, celebrated every year on January 15. The inspiration this very special man gave to the world will surely live on in history for many generations to come.

INDEX